I0087563

Joy Ridderhof

Voice Catcher Around the World

Rebecca Davis

Potter's Wheel Books
Showing children the Master Potter at work
Greenville, South Carolina

Joy Ridderhof : voice catcher around the world / by Rebecca Davis.

Summary: A biography for children of the first "audio" missionary.

Ridderhof, Joy, 1903-1984.

Joy Ridderhof: Voice Catcher Around the World
Christian biography
Juvenile nonfiction / Biography and autobiography / Religious
ages 7-10

All Scripture quotations are from the King James Version of the Bible.

Cover design by Tim Davis

© 2015 Rebecca Davis
Potter's Wheel Books
Greenville, SC 29609
www.hiddenheroesmissionarystories.com

ISBN: 0692382488
ISBN-13: 978-0692382486

To my mother,
who always encouraged me
to read biographies,
trusting that they would eventually
do me some good

Other books in the Potter's Wheel series
Fanny Crosby: Queen of Gospel Songs

Other books by Rebecca Davis
With Daring Faith: A Biography of Amy Carmichael
George Mueller: A Father to the Fatherless

the Hidden Heroes series
True Stories of God at Work Around the World
***
#1 With Two Hands
Stories of God at Work in Ethiopia
***
#2 The Good News Must Go Out
Stories of God at Work in the Central African Republic
***
#3 Witness Men
True Stories of God at Work in Papua, Indonesia
***
#4 Return of the White Book
True Stories of God at Work in Southeast Asia
***
#5 Lights in a Dark Place
True Stories of God at Work in Colombia
***
#6 Living Water in the Desert
True Stories of God at Work in Iran

For more information, visit
www.hiddenheroesmissionarystories.com
or the Facebook page
Hidden Heroes Missionary Stories

Contents

Chapter 1

My Name is Joy

Joy scooted her chair away from the little desk in her bedroom. She bent over with that hard pain in her stomach. It hurt so much.

"Oh, Ann," the teenage girl groaned. "I just won't be able to make it through the tests. I just can't survive them."

Churning, churning. Her stomach wouldn't stop churning!

Joy's friend, Ann Sherwood, smiled at her from the floor where she was sitting cross-legged, studying. "You'll make it, Joy," she said. "You always do."

"Sometimes I'm afraid I'm going to throw up with worrying about my grades," Joy said.

"Worrying is probably bad for your stomach," Ann observed.

"But I have to!" Joy protested. "If I didn't worry, that would mean I didn't care about doing well. And I care a whole bunch! I want to please God with my life. And right now that means school."

"Well, I do too," answered Ann. "Do you suppose I ought to worry as much as you do?"

"Ohhh, I don't know." Joy groaned and flopped onto her bed. "Oh, I just want the tests to be over."

Before long, those tests were over, and Joy did well on them, as she always did. Then came a new challenge.

"Oh, Ann," Joy groaned as they walked home

from school. "I can't believe I actually have to speak in front of a school assembly. Maybe I'll get a terrible disease and be too sick to do it."

"Well, the way you worry, you'll be too sick to do it without the terrible disease," Ann answered. They turned the corner and walked up the sidewalk of Witmer Street to Joy's home in Los Angeles.

"I can't do it. I absolutely cannot do it," Joy muttered. "That's just all there is to it. I'm going to get dizzy and break out in a sweat. I'll faint, right in front of all those students and parents and teachers. I can't bear it, Ann!"

"Well, you believe the Lord will help you, don't you?" said Ann.

"Oh, I ask Him to help me all the time. Absolutely all the time. *Please help me,* I pray. Over and over. Of course I do! But you know He expects us to do our best. He wants us to use all the skills we have and all that. I want to do my best, I just want to do a good job, and that's why I worry so much. Maybe I won't do my best. Oh, I can't stand it!"

Ann nodded and waved good-bye as Joy climbed the steps into her home.

Why did she worry so much? Surely it was just because she wanted to do well.

And then came the day when she stood up to speak in front of the assembly. She felt sick, she felt as if she were going to faint, but she got through it.

Surely worrying wasn't wrong—surely it showed that she cared about doing a good job!

But one thing Joy had to admit was wrong was how impatient and disrespectful she was. *I'm a Christian,* she thought. *This isn't the way Christians are supposed to act.* She kept feeling sorry after she did it. But she kept doing it. Day after day, the

Christian life seemed like such a dreary struggle to this teenage girl.

My name is Joy, she thought. *But I never feel it.* She looked out the window at the bright blue California sky. *It always feels gray and cloudy in my heart.*

And so day after day passed, plodding on. Trying so hard to be good. Always failing. "I've got to just try harder," she said with determination. "I'll try harder to live the kind of life I know a good Christian should live."

But it was never enough. She always failed to be the Christian she should be.

Then a day came that changed Joy's life. It was in 1920, when Joy was seventeen.

The speaker in her church was a man she'd never heard of. She opened her Bible, and the man began to speak about the very problem she struggled with. Worry.

"If you worry, you're not trusting God," the speaker said. "Jesus told His disciples that they shouldn't even worry about what to eat or drink! He told them that if they worried, then *their faith was small.*"

How terrible! *I knew that my impatience and disrespect were wrong,* she thought, *but I had no idea that my worry was wrong too. I'm just hopeless!*

Joy felt the familiar old knot in her stomach again. She couldn't help but worry about her worrying. She felt dizzy and sick.

But the speaker wasn't finished.

"There's a way to be saved from your worry. A great man, George Mueller, once said,

'The beginning of worry is the end of faith.

And the beginning of true faith is the end of worry.' "

True faith is the end of worry, Joy thought. *Does that mean if I have true faith I won't ever need to worry?*

"True faith in the truly powerful God will bring an end to your worry," the speaker added. "He loves you! He loves you! Repent of your worrying and turn to Christ. He can fill you with His joy."

Joy had never heard anything like it in all her life! "I will do it, O Lord," she murmured in prayer. "I'll stop excusing my worry. I'll stop pretending it's a good thing. It's wrong. I'll trust that You can bring good out of anything. Even my own foolishness."

Joy listened to this speaker every night all week. At the end of the week she went to meet him. Dr. Robert McQuilkin.

"Dr. McQuilkin!" she said, her heart pounding. "Somebody was saying that you're thinking about starting a Bible school?"

"Yes," he said, shaking her hand. "Back in South Carolina. That's my home state."

South Carolina! That's over two thousand miles away! It would take days to get there on the train! The trip would be so expensive!

"I'd like to study there." Joy was surprised to hear those words come out of her mouth.

Dr. McQuilkin's kind eyes looked into hers. "The Lord will guide you," he said.

The Lord will guide me? He will? Joy asked the Lord for help all the time, for the tests she had to take and speeches she had to give, and other hard things she had to do, but she had never even thought about asking the Lord for help in making a decision.

The Lord will guide me?

A new kind of joy began to bubble inside her.

The Lord will guide me!

Chapter 2

A Different Kind of Love

Joy finished high school, trusting and praying. And rejoicing! Whenever she started to feel that old knot of worry in her stomach, she started rejoicing and praising God. Finally high school was over. All the testing and speech-giving were finally done.

How will I be able to get to South Carolina to Columbia Bible School?

Never mind. The Lord will guide me.

And then Joy's married sister wrote her a letter. She lived oh-so-far away in Minnesota.

Dear Joy,

Now that I have two little ones, I sure could use some help! Would you come and stay with me for a few weeks after you finish high school? I'll pay your way from California to up here in Minnesota, and then back home again.

This was it. This was the answer.

"I'd be glad to come," Joy wrote back, but instead of paying my way back to California, would you pay it all the way to South Carolina?"

And her sister had done it. Just like that.

Joy spent a pleasant few weeks with her sister and her children. Then she took the train to South Carolina. She was going to be one of the first five students in the new Columbia Bible School. It was 1923.

God had guided her. And Joy didn't need to worry even one little bit. Instead, she rejoiced and trusted.

৵৹৵

The two years at Columbia Bible School passed by so quickly. For part of that time, Joy lived with the McQuilkin family. She watched their joyful faith, even in times of great sorrow. Her life was forever changed.

Now it was finally time to leave the United States for mission work. In 1930, when Joy was 27 years old, Ann Sherwood and some others came to say good-bye. Joy stood high up on the ship headed down the coast of California.

The ship sailed away, down past the coast of Mexico to Central America, to the country of Honduras.

Finally she arrived in the strange, dirty capital city. "I won't worry! I'll trust God!" Joy sang in her heart.

A few missionaries were already there. They welcomed Joy. "Look at our phonograph machine," one missionary said proudly.

"Yes, we have one of those back home," Joy said. "But the machine we have is very big. I love these smaller ones." She held up the black record and looked at it. "When I was little, my father found out that the records he had bought played silly songs and love songs. He got rid of them!"

"But this one plays hymns and gospel songs," the missionary answered gladly.

"Does it play them in Spanish?" Joy asked. That was the language of her new country.

"No, there aren't any records that play hymns in Spanish as far as I know," came the reply. "I wish there were! But these phonograph machines are all over the country, even in the small villages. They play silly songs and love songs, as you say. They're a big distraction to the people when we want to give them the gospel. But at least here in the mission house we can use them to listen to good music."

ॐॐ

Joy traveled with a partner to many little villages in Honduras. Finally she became confident that the little village of Marcala was the place God wanted her to live. Joy and her new friend Cruzita clip-clopped on their mules to the little village. They were ready to stay for months or even years.

Like all the other villages, the central market of Marcala was filled with grass-topped stalls. Here the people sold their vegetables and fruits and breads and shawls and other goods. Half-wild dogs with skinny ribs wandered in and out through the market stalls, hoping to find a bit of meat or a scrap of bread to steal.

Joy watched as the Catholic priest strode through the little streets of the village. He was a fearsome sight, with his long black robe and long black beard. Everyone bowed and greeted him as "father." They were obviously afraid of him.

Joy and Cruzita clip-clopped past the saloon, the place where people went to get drunk. Just inside the saloon they could see a man sitting next to a phonograph machine. He turned the handle round and round to make the screechy record play the noisy Spanish music.

"My mama told me not to fall in love," the man's voice sang on the record. "But when I see a young woman, I turn to look."

Joy shook her head. *These people are so poor. How can such poor people get those machines?* What a distraction those records and those songs were to the gospel!

She had a much better love story to give them.

Their first Sunday morning in Marcala, Joy and Cruzita walked into the town square. Joy lifted her accordion to her shoulder. Cruzita pulled out her tambourine and began to shake it. "Listen! Listen!" they called.

The few Christians from the village gathered with them. Together they began to sing from the new Spanish hymn book, a gospel song in Spanish.

I love to hear the story which angel voices tell,
How once the King of glory
came down on earth to dwell.
I am both weak and sinful; but this I surely know,
The Lord came down to save me,
because He loved me so.

People began to pour out of the markets and stalls and shops and huts. Someone even turned off the phonograph in the saloon! They wanted to hear this strange woman from the far-off United States. Here she was, singing with Cruzita and those people from their own village that were gathered around.

God loved them? Was this what they really believed? It was a new thought!

Joy and Cruzita found a place to live in Marcala. They made a home there. Joy hired a woman to help her with the cooking and cleaning.

Before long, the Lord began to show Himself strong in this little village.

"What's the matter with your son?" Joy asked her cook one day. Something was clearly wrong with Juan, but Joy couldn't understand what it was.

"Oh, Miss Joy," the cook replied, "he is sick in his body and his soul. We don't know how to help him. He won't eat, and he grows so thin. Sometimes he cries out, and we don't even know why."

"How long has he been this way?" asked Joy.

"Years. He's becoming so thin, he will die, I think. And he is so miserable all the time! What can we do?"

Immediately Joy heard in her heart the voice of Dr. McQuilkin.

"Rejoice, even when things are hard," she said. "Don't give up. God can heal his body and heal his soul. Let's pray and praise God!"

Joy and her cook and Cruzita and some others praised God for His great ability to heal and show His mighty power. They prayed for God to show His mighty work in Juan's life.

And Juan was healed! He became cheerful and well, eager to work!

The news spread like fire around the village of Marcala. "Did you hear? Did you see? The crazy sick boy isn't crazy and sick anymore! Those new people—the ones who talk about Jesus and God's love—they did it!"

Juan became one of the first new Christians in Marcala. Before long he went off to work for another missionary family in another village.

"Did you hear? Did you hear what happened to Juan?" More and more people came to listen to Joy and Cruzita and the others read to them from the Bible and tell them that Jesus had died for them.

But the priest became very angry that someone was teaching a religion that pulled people away from his authority.

Chapter 3

The Priest Wants to Kill You!

Don Pedro was one of the most important men in Marcala. But now he sat in the chair in the mission house, squeezing his hands.

Joy and another missionary with her waited for Don Pedro to speak

Don Pedro cleared his throat. "I know the priest is angry that you have come to live here," he began. "I watch him go stomping down the street with his big black robe flying behind him. He warns everyone, 'Stay away from those women with the black books!' But I also know that the priest is not a good man. So I asked myself, 'What could be so bad about what those women say?' And I've listened. The priest talks only about God's anger, but I like what you say about God's love. I like what you say about Jesus."

Don Pedro paused, searching for the right words. Joy and Arthur, the other missionary, sat silent, listening. "I would like to know," Don Pedro finally said, "what I can do to make God be pleased with me. How can I pay for my sins?"

The missionaries glanced at each other. They knew Don Pedro was asking the wrong question.

"Don Pedro," Arthur began, "you can't do anything to make God be pleased with you."

Don Pedro just looked at him. He knew that these new missionaries talked very differently from the priest. They talked a lot about the love of God and the death of Jesus Christ for our sins. But he still didn't understand.

"Don Pedro," Joy said. "God's Word, the Bible, talks about this in the book of Titus. 'Not by works of righteousness that we have done, but according to His mercy He saved us—' "

Don Pedro held up his hand. "But I must do works of righteousness," he said. "That's the only way to reach God. I know I need to reach Him. I know I'm far from Him."

"No," Arthur replied. "Jesus Christ has already done all the works of righteousness that need to be done for us to reach God. Listen." He read from II Corinthians 5:21. "'He has made Him to be sin for us, who knew no sin, so that we could be made the righteousness of God in Him.' Jesus has already done it all for us. He is the only sacrifice that we need."

Don Pedro shook his head slowly. "This is hard to believe," he said. "It seems too good to be true."

21

"That's why it's called the gospel!" Joy cried out, clapping her hands. "It's good news!"

For several hours Joy and Arthur talked and prayed with Don Pedro. Finally Don Pedro bowed in prayer with them. He asked to receive God's full and free forgiveness for his sins. His whole expression changed, and he said, "God has accepted me!"

Don Pedro's life was transformed. Now he wanted to read the Bible and learn about Jesus and worship God alone. Now he determined he wouldn't live with someone that he wasn't married to. This was very surprising news to the people of Marcala.

The priest was furious! Was that foreign woman going to turn the whole village over to her religion? He hired two men to kill Joy late at night.

Every night Joy walked with one of her

students to the student's home. Then she walked back to her own home . . . alone in the dark. One night the two killers hid behind bushes to shoot Joy as she came back alone.

That night, the young girl's parents said, "Miss Joy, will you stay the night here tonight? We have to go away, and we don't want to leave our children alone."

"Gladly!" said Joy. She had no idea that two men were waiting outside for her to return to her own house, so they could kill her. But she didn't leave her student's house all night.

"Miss Joy, Miss Joy!" someone said the next day. "Did you know that two men were planning to kill you last night? They were talking about it in the saloon!"

"No, I had no idea," said Joy. "But God knew. He protected me!"

The two men never again tried to kill Joy.

But the priest himself tried to kill Don Pedro.

One day Joy played her accordion outside for the people, the way she often did. Don Pedro stood near her, ready to preach to the people who were gathered.

But at the edge of the crowd, the priest quietly stood. He pulled out a gun and pointed it at Don Pedro.

Another man saw the gun and grabbed it away from the priest.

"You won't stop me!" the priest snarled. He stomped forward and grabbed Don Pedro's collar. "You come with me!" he shouted.

A crowd of people gathered, watching.

Dragging Don Pedro by the collar, the priest stomped off to the cathedral. The crowd of people followed him, afraid. What was he going to do?

The priest stopped in front of the statue of

Mary. "Bow down!" he cried. "Bow down and worship the Blessed Mother!"

But Don Pedro didn't bow. "I will worship no one but the true God and His Son Jesus Christ," he answered firmly.

The priest was furious. He grabbed a crucifix off the wall and banged Don Pedro over the head with it. Don Pedro stumbled backward. His head began to bleed.

The crowd gasped. The priest had used a crucifix to hit someone? A murmur of anger arose in the crowd.

The priest stepped back. "Get out!" he yelled. "All of you!"

Don Pedro stumbled out with the others. Then he went back to see Joy.

"We'll rejoice," Joy said as she tenderly bandaged the wound. "Our Lord Jesus allowed you to suffer for His great Name."

News spread quickly of what the priest had done and how the Christians responded. More and more people came to hear about the power of Jesus Christ.

This wasn't the only time the Christians of Marcala suffered for their faith. When times were dangerous, sometimes dozens of people came to stay inside the walls of the mission house, because it was safe there.

One day Joy looked around at all the people. *How will we feed all these people?* she wondered. *Farmers aren't traveling the roads now.*

All the Christians gathered to pray. "I remember stories from a man named George Mueller," she told them. "He fed a lot of orphans, and always trusted God to give them enough food, and He always did. So this is what we'll do. We'll rejoice! We'll rejoice that our God is a great God who always hears our prayers! We'll rejoice that He shows Himself strong in a time of need! We'll rejoice that He'll supply the food we need!"

All around her, the Christians began to rejoice and praise God. They knew He had promised to take care of them, and He was going to do exactly that.

"All right, brothers and sisters," Joy declared. "We trust God for the answer, and we must watch for it. Just like the farmer who asked for rain and got out his umbrella. Keep watching."

Joy looked out the door of the mission house. There on the road, she could see someone riding a mule, coming toward them. "That must be our answer!" she called.

It was.

On the mule was Juan, the boy who had been healed, who had gone to work for another missionary family.

"Hello, Miss Joy!" he called, waving his hat. "I'm coming with food!"

He approached closer and climbed off the mule.

"The family I work for—they said, 'God is telling us to send lots of food to Miss Joy.' So here I am, to bring it to you. God protected me along the road."

"God used you to answer our prayer, Juan!" Joy said. "Before we even prayed, God was answering our prayer. Rejoice with us!"

Chapter 4

The Voice that Never Gets Tired

Joy sat and stared out the window.

Instead of seeing the little grass-roofed huts of Marcala, she saw skyscrapers.

Instead of hearing squawking chickens and barking dogs, she heard cars honking at each other.

She was back in Los Angeles again. How could it be?

For six years she had worked in Honduras. What a wonderful time it had been! How many people she had seen trust in Jesus and give their lives to Him in joyful service!

But now, in 1936, she had to return home. It hardly felt like home anymore.

She had no energy. She could barely even do anything. This awful disease would take months for her to recover from.

"Dear God," she prayed. "I know I must rejoice in everything. I do rejoice in this hard time. I know You're going to do something great out of it. But it's hard, Lord." She sighed.

"But I do believe You. I do believe You're doing the best thing for me now. Please show me what You want me to learn."

In her dreams and her daydreams Joy kept thinking about Marcala. She thought about Don Pedro and his strong prayers to the God who loved him. She thought about Juan with his quick smile and willing hands. How happy she had been to see him clip-clopping on his mule with his packs full of food in answer to their prayers!

She thought about brave Cruzita, who had stood against men who had come to threaten them at the mission house.

Joy sighed again. She thought about an old woman in the mountains she had gone to visit. The woman couldn't read, so Joy didn't leave a Bible with her. Instead, Joy had tried to help her memorize some Bible verses. But the woman just became confused, and couldn't learn them. "How can I rejoice about that, Lord?" Joy asked. Her sighs changed to deep trembling breaths. She thought she was going to cry.

In her dreams Joy heard those old phonographs playing those silly songs in the saloons.

The cockroach, the cockroach
Can't walk anymore
Because he doesn't have, because he's lacking
His main walking leg.

31

What a ridiculous song, Joy thought. *Why do they sing such ridiculous songs?*

And yet as she turned over in bed, the tune kept running through her mind.

If only there were records that played gospel songs in Spanish. She remembered that another missionary had said something about that.

Phonograph records. Phonograph records to play stories and songs about the gospel. In Spanish.

What if that old woman in the mountains had had a phonograph? What if she had a record that told the gospel, a record that she could play over and over and over? Then the old woman could hear the same stories and songs again and again, until she understood them. A phonograph record could stay with her always. It wouldn't get tired of saying the same things over and over!

"I guess I can learn to play the guitar even

while I'm sick," Joy said. "It will give me something to do. Then when I'm feeling better, I can make a gospel recording, and I can sing some songs for it."

The idea began to grow in her heart. She wrote letters to friends. "Please pray with me about this," she said. "I think the Lord may want me to make some Spanish gospel recordings."

When some friends visited her, Joy told them about her idea. "But how will you make the recording?" someone asked. "You don't even have any recording equipment."

"I don't know," Joy admitted. "The equipment is big and very expensive. I wouldn't know how to use it even if I did have it! But the Lord knows all that, and I trust Him."

Joy's days in bed began to seem brighter. "Let's see," she planned. "I'll read some Bible verses in Spanish on the recording, and explain them. Then I'll sing a cheery gospel song that the Christians in Honduras know. . . . Lord, this is so exciting!"

Finally when Joy was feeling a little better, the time was right. Someone let her use his recording studio. Friends helped out. Joy made one simple recording. When she held the record in her hands, she felt a great thrill of accomplishment.

"This is so wonderful! I could actually do something for You while I have to be back home getting well! Thank You, Lord!"

Joy mailed out several copies of the recording. Some to Don Pedro in Marcala. Some to other missionary friends in Honduras. And a few to other people.

"I want to do another one, Lord," she murmured. "When I go back to Marcala, I hope I can have several different records to play. They'll have different messages and different songs. I wonder how they'll like the one I sent them?"

Joy waited days and weeks to hear back from her faraway friends. She waited the long time that it took for the records to travel from California to Honduras. She waited the long time that it took for letters to travel back from Honduras to her in California.

"All the people love the records!" the missionaries and other Christians wrote. "They love these gospel recordings! Not just the Christians—everyone! They play them on the phonographs over and over! They're memorizing the songs and the Bible verses!"

Every letter Joy received, from every missionary, all said the same thing. "The records are wonderful! They are a gift from God!"

Joy could hardly eat, she was so thrilled. "This is wonderful, this is so wonderful, Lord!" she said. "Now I can see why I was rejoicing!

35

Sometimes I can't see it, but this time You showed it to me! You showed me the reason I had to come back here and be sick for a while. Oh, Lord, this is so wonderful. Thank You, thank You!"

She made another recording and then made copies of it and sent them off. And another. She asked Mexicans and other Spanish speakers in California to help her.

More letters came, from more missionaries who had heard the records and borrowed them. "The records keep giving the gospel message, long after we have to leave!" they wrote. "The records never get tired! They can keep preaching to the crowd, even when we need to speak to people one on one!"

Other missionaries from other Spanish-speaking countries wrote letters to her too. "We've heard about your Spanish gospel recordings," they wrote. "We'd like to order some for our mission work." Joy began sending records out not just to Honduras, but to many countries. There were three hundred million Spanish-speaking people in the world. That meant a lot of records!

Joy kept working faster and harder, making one recording after another. She sent out records to all the people who wrote to her asking for them. She felt filled with energy and excitement.

"Hey!" she noticed one day. "I have just as much energy as when I first went to Marcala! That means I'm well! I can finally go back there, where I belong! Thank You, Lord!"

Chapter 5

Other Sheep, Lord?

It was 1939, and Joy had been back in California for three years. With great delight, she began to prepare for her return to Honduras. Honduras . . . and Marcala! She could hardly wait to see Don Pedro again. And Cruzita, and Juan, and oh, so many others!

She just wanted to finish making fifty Spanish gospel recordings. That was a lot, but she could do it. And just think, when she returned to Marcala, she would have all those different records! What excellent helpers those records would be!

Everything had turned out just right, and her heart sang. It was so clear why she had been called to stay in the U.S. for a time. It was for those Spanish gospel recordings.

But then Joy received a letter.

When she first read it, she felt confused. This couldn't be what the Lord wanted, could it?

Dear Madam,

We have heard of your Spanish Gospel Recordings, and we praise God for them. We are missionaries to the Navajo Indians. We are asking you to make some records in the Navajo language. We can come to your studio, and a Navajo Christian can come with us. He can speak the gospel messages on your records. We will pay for everything.

We will look forward to your reply.

This couldn't be what the Lord wanted. No, no! Why, if she helped someone do records in the Navajo language, then there would be someone else asking for another language. Then someone else would ask for another, and then, well, who knows! There might be hundreds of languages in the world, for all she knew!

"Lord, you know I'm supposed to go back to Honduras," Joy said out loud. "I'm getting ready to go! I need to go back!"

Joy looked around her little bedroom. All around her lay boxes of letters. They thanked her for the Spanish gospel records. They praised God for what He was doing through the records. They sent money to help pay for the records. They asked her to send more records.

In the corner on the desk sat the old typewriter where she banged out answers to the letters. It was almost hidden by papers and boxes. All around her sat boxes of records ready to be shipped to different Spanish-speaking missionaries.

But this was the first letter to ask for a different language.

"I can't do it." Joy sat down hard on the edge of her bed and held that letter with both hands. "If I start this, where will it end? When will I get back to Honduras?"

But Joy recognized God's voice.

What about My other sheep, Joy?

Joy remembered when Jesus said, "I have other sheep that are not of this fold. I have to bring them too."

"I know, Lord," she said out loud. "You love Your sheep all over the world. And I do too. Not just the Spanish-speaking ones."

Joy felt a strange feeling in her stomach. Something was going to change here.

Will I do what the Lord wants, even if it means I can't go back to Marcala just yet?

"Lord," she said finally, "I'll make recordings

in as many languages as You want me to. And I'll rejoice about it. I'll wait to return to Honduras."

Somehow Joy had a hunch that she had just opened the door to all the languages in the world. "I trust You, Lord," she said.

The missionaries came with their Navajo friend and made the records. With great joy they left to play their records for the native people.

Then Joy received another letter.

Dear Joy,

We haven't seen each other since you left for Honduras ten years ago, I know. But I have to come back home to take care of Mama in the last days of her life. I would love to visit you!

Love, Ann Sherwood

Ann! Joy's best friend in school! My, she hadn't seen her since 1930. But now she was coming! She would rejoice with Joy in all the gospel recordings Joy had been able to make.

Ann walked with Joy up the steps to Joy's little room. She listened to Joy bubble over with excitement about God's work through the gospel recordings. "It's so exciting what the Lord is doing!" Joy said. "Let's see, I need to find a letter I got just yesterday from a missionary in a little village in Mexico. . . ."

Ann watched as Joy rummaged around looking for the letter. She looked past Joy, all around the little bedroom. She saw the stacks of letters here and there. She saw the boxes filled with records waiting to be labelled. She saw the typewriter with a half-written letter in it.

"Joy," she said gently. "Would you like to have some help with this work?"

Joy looked up in surprise.

"I think I could come over a couple of days a week," Ann said. "I can help get your papers organized. I can even answer some of the letters. Then you'd have more time to prepare for your recordings and the other things you want to do."

Joy clapped her hands in delight. "Ann, I don't even need to work at rejoicing about that one! I'm so happy I could jump up and down right here!"

৯৩

As time passed, Ann began to spend more and more time working with Joy. She organized the papers and even wrote some of the music for some of the gospel recordings.

"Ann, I can't possibly pay you for everything you're doing for me!" Joy said one day. "How in the world will you manage?"

"Well, how in the world do you manage?" asked Ann.

"I just manage by trusting the Lord," Joy began. She scratched her head as she looked around at the crowded bedroom. "I trust the Lord to send me what I need, and He always does. It isn't much, but it's enough."

"Well, I can manage the same way you do," Ann replied. "So it's settled. I'll keep working with you, and keep trusting the Lord with you."

One evening the two ladies prepared to head out to the recording studio together. There they would meet the Spanish-speaking Christians who would help them make their next recording.

"I always take enough with me to pay on the spot," Joy had explained to Ann. "I don't ever want to go into debt. I don't ever make an appointment until I have enough money for it."

Joy pulled out her purse to make sure the money was all there. "Let's see here." She paused.

"What's wrong?" Ann asked.

"It isn't enough. It isn't even half enough." Joy opened her purse wider and began to dig down to the bottom. "I must have miscounted before. Could I have laid some money somewhere else?" She looked up. Her eyes darted here and there around the little house.

Ann looked and replied, "No, that's for sure all the money we have. Should we cancel?"

"No, we can't cancel! The speakers and singers are coming. The studio is reserved." Joy set her mouth. "We have to do it. The Lord will provide. We'll rejoice that this is an opportunity for us to trust Him. Maybe someone will come in in the middle of the recording session. Maybe one of the Spanish singers will give some money. Maybe even the man who runs the studio will want to give something!"

Joy and Ann set off. Both of them were excited to see how the Lord would provide. Excited . . . and maybe a little scared.

The recording went well. The singers sounded beautiful. The preaching was passionate.

But no one offered to give any money.

Finally the recording time ended. The studio director pulled out his book and his pencil and sat down at his desk. He began to figure up the exact amount Joy owed. Joy looked around as the Spanish singers packed up their guitars and walked out the door.

The studio director kept figuring. He added and subtracted numbers from all the different payments Joy had made through the months. He erased and wrote again. His brow creased in concentration.

Joy and Ann looked at each other. Ann shrugged.

Please, Lord, Joy thought. *What will I tell him?*

Finally the studio director looked up.

"Miss Ridderhof," he said, "I've made a mistake in the books. I overcharged you on two of your other recording sessions. This recording session tonight will be free, and I owe you some money."

Joy and Ann looked at each other again. Ann raised her eyebrows and made a funny face.

"Praise God!" Joy whispered. "He always provides!"

๛

Ann Sherwood stayed with Gospel Recordings for over forty years, serving God. He always provided.

Chapter 6

Only a Thousand Miles More

"Won't it be wonderful, Ann? Won't it be just glorious?" Even though Joy was forty years old, she was so happy she felt like skipping.

"Yes, it will be wonderful," Ann answered cautiously. "But how will we get the gasoline to get there?"

"God will do it! He will do it! Oh, I'm rejoicing already!"

By 1943 Joy and Ann had opened their own little recording studio, in a shed behind Joy's house. Other people had joined them in the work. They had recorded the gospel in several languages. They had even recorded one tribal group who had no Bible at all! It was a thrilling event to watch the tribal man listening to the words in Spanish and then speaking them in his own language into the recording machine.

And now they'd received a letter asking them to make another gospel recording. It was for another tribe with no Bible.

But this time, for the first time, they were going to leave the United States to do it.

"This is a new step, a step of faith," Joy said. "Don't you see? There are so, so many tribes out there who don't have the gospel of Jesus Christ in their own language! The missionaries haven't even learned the languages yet!"

Ann looked thoughtful. "I know. Well, the Mazahua Indians weren't allowed to cross over from Mexico to California. We know that God has a reason for that."

"Yes, well, it's because there's a war on," Joy answered. "But God will make a way for us to take our first trip out of the country ourselves. The first trip out for the organization called Gospel Recordings! You and me! And we got that portable phonograph as a gift, and oh! I can hardly contain my joy!"

Ann smiled at Joy's enthusiasm as they approached the official-looking building. Because of the war, they had to get permission for everything. They even had to get permission to buy the gas they'd need for the car to drive to Mexico.

The officer behind the window looked disgusted. "You women can't have any more gasoline tickets!" he said. "Don't you know there's a war on? Going into Mexico for *what?*"

Joy's voice sounded small. "To take the gospel to people who have never heard. You know, the story of Jesus—"

"I know, I know," the officer interrupted impatiently. "I can see you already have too many gasoline tickets. You're getting way too many. I'm going to reduce your number."

Joy stepped back as if he had slapped her. She needed *more* gasoline tickets for traveling to Mexico, but he was taking some away!

Silently, Joy and Ann walked away from the office together. Joy didn't feel like skipping.

"I just need to get alone and pray, Ann," she said. "I need to ask God, was I trying to go too fast, to move ahead of Him? I thought the gas tickets would be the easy part. I expected we'd be spending our time praying for the car."

Yes, they still needed a car to drive to Mexico. A big car—big enough to carry all the heavy equipment they needed to take with them.

Joy knelt down by her bed. "I will rejoice, Lord. I do rejoice. You're always faithful, and

You're always on time." She paused. "You remember, of course, that we have to leave in three days." She paused again. "The missionaries and the tribal people will all be waiting for us."

Joy turned to Psalm 16:11, one of her favorite Scriptures. "Thou wilt show me the path of life: in thy presence is fullness of joy; at thy right hand there are pleasures for evermore."

"Lord Jesus," she prayed, "You will give us fullness of joy. We trust You to do Your work."

A little tap-tap came on the door.

"Yes?"

Ann came in. "Joy, you'll never guess what just happened."

Joy smiled. "That nasty gas-ticket man came here and gave us all the gas tickets we need."

"Well, not exactly," answered Ann. "But you need to be sitting down when you hear this. We have the car we need—one that's big enough!"

Joy clapped her hands. "That's wonderful! God gave us the car!" Then she stopped. "But we still don't have the tickets."

"But there's more," said Ann. "God has done it all! The man who's lending us the car has plenty of gas tickets. He's giving us all we need!"

"I knew it!" Joy jumped up from where she was kneeling. "I knew it, Ann! I rejoiced because I knew God was going to do something big! Let's rejoice together!"

Together Joy and Ann drove the two thousand miles to Mexico City. There in a recording studio that God provided, they met the little barefoot tribal men. The men listened to the missionaries speak the gospel in simple Spanish sentences. Then they translated the words into the tribal language that no one yet understood.

The tribal men had never even known that such things as recordings existed. But now they listened to the recording of their own voices. They heard their own voices telling them about the true God and His Son, Jesus Christ. They stood with their mouths hanging open at the sound of their own voices speaking these astounding words.

Watching from another room, Joy squeezed her hands together. "This is what I was made for, Ann," she whispered. "This is what God wants me to do all my life."

When Joy had a chance, she asked the missionaries, "Are there more tribal people around here who don't have the Bible in their own language?"

"Oh, dozens of them!" came the answer.

That was all Joy needed to hear. She and Ann stayed in Mexico for months. They recorded first one tribal language and then another. In each tribe, the missionary found a person who could understand some Spanish to bring to the recording studio. Then the missionary would read one sentence of the gospel message in Spanish. Then the tribal person translated it into his own language. On and on they went until the whole message had been given.

After several months, Joy and Ann had recorded the beautiful story of the gospel in over thirty tribal languages. More tribes were hearing how the true God had sent His Son Jesus Christ to die for us so that we could have life in Him. Most of these tribes had never before had a gospel witness in their own language.

So amazing. So beautiful. Over and over Joy realized that tears of joy were in her eyes. Her heart was singing.

"Ann," Joy said one day, "we can't go back to California without visiting my village in Honduras. It isn't that much farther."

Ann laughed. "It's only a thousand miles more!"

"Yes, see?" said Joy. "It's not that much farther. And we've already come so far. We can do it."

They finished recording thirty-three tribal languages in Mexico. Then they drove the thousand miles to Marcala.

And there were the people of the village! It had been eight years since Joy had seen them. But they gathered around her to welcome her back.

"Miss Joy! Miss Joy!" they called. "Welcome home!"

Joy laughed and cried at the same time. She hugged all of them. "Oh friends, have you enjoyed the Spanish gospel records I sent you?"

"Yes, yes! We love them!" they all cried. People that Joy didn't even know said, "I came to Jesus Christ because of those records!"

Joy held out her arms as if she wanted to hug everybody at once. "My friends, I can't stay long," she said. "God has called me to a wider work." She told them about the thirty-three tribal languages she and Ann had just recorded. Then she talked to them about the many other tribes out there, somewhere, around the world. She didn't even know how many.

"He has other sheep, right? We have to do what we can to reach them all, yes?"

"Yes!" said her friends in Marcala. "You have to go back to your place and do your work. You can help bring in those other sheep. We rejoice with you!"

Chapter 7

Praying Every Wednesday?

One day in 1947 Joy made a phone call back to Los Angeles. She was far away, at a prayer conference in Washington. But right now she had something important she needed to say.

"Hello!" Joy said into the telephone, "how is everyone doing back there?" Ann wasn't the only one working at the little house on Witmer Street now. Now there was a whole team of volunteers, all working together. They answered the many letters and set up recording sessions. They planned the scripts and kept that equipment working. They made copies of the records and packed them up for shipping. They drove here and there all over town to make sure all the work got done. Every team member was busy all the time.

"Oh, Joy," answered Doris, one of the new young team members. "There's so much to do! We can't possibly get it all done!"

"Listen, Doris," Joy spoke clearly into the telephone. "This is really important. I heard a speaker at this prayer conference. He inspired me again, like Dr. McQuilkin—oh, there's so much to tell you about when I get back home! But the main thing is this: remember that we need to rejoice and pray. Pray without ceasing! Prayer is the most important part of all that we do."

"Yes, we do pray every day," Doris replied into the telephone.

"But now we need to start taking a day off for prayer every week," Joy continued. "I want all of you to take every Wednesday, and just pray all day."

"Really?" Doris said. "But—"

Joy quickly added, "You can't do all the work anyway. So you might just as well pray. The Lord will do it through you."

Doris hung up the phone in a daze. She walked to the other room where all her team members were working frantically.

"Everybody, you won't believe what Joy just told me," she said.

"What?" someone asked.

"We're supposed to take every Wednesday off just to pray."

The work stopped as everyone stared at Doris.

"*Every* Wednesday?"

"All day?"

"We already can't do everything we're

supposed to do! How in the world can we get it done if we take off an entire day?"

"That's tomorrow," someone said. "We'd better do it."

Every work day always started with prayer. But this time it was different. Everyone knew that the entire Wednesday was to be devoted to prayer. They needed to start even while Joy was gone.

They prayed together.

Then someone read a Scripture.

Then they sang.

They praised God, and praised Him and praised Him, for all He had done and all He was going to do.

They prayed some more, asking God to do His work through them.

They read more Scripture.

Then they praised God, and praised Him and

praised Him, for all He had done and all He was going to do. Then they prayed some more.

For the whole day the team prayed and sang and prayed and rejoiced and prayed and read the Bible. They just focused on the Lord. It was a time of great blessing and joy.

But when the day was over, there was all the work, still waiting to be done.

How could they do this every week?

Joy returned from her trip. "No matter how much work piles up, this is what we're doing," she said firmly. "You know, we can work and work and work, and do it all for the Lord. But if the Lord isn't doing the work, nothing truly important will be accomplished."

Everyone nodded. They knew it was true.

Every Wednesday they prayed. Week after week. Month after month.

One day Ann said, "Have you noticed that we're getting just as much done every week?"

"I've seen it!" said Doris. "We might even be doing a little better!"

"And you know what else?" said Joy. "We're doing it without worrying. We're doing it with rejoicing!"

"No more bending over double with stomach pain, right, Joy?" asked Ann.

"Absolutely not!" Joy laughed. "No more stomach pain, not for years now! This is the Lord's work, not ours!"

Not long after, Joy made another startling announcement.

"I believe the Lord wants us to give away the records instead of selling them," she said.

Again, everyone in the room looked at her. "*Give* them away?" someone said. "We don't charge very much for them as it is!"

"The records cost something for us to produce, you know, Joy," said one man. "It only makes sense to ask—"

Joy held up her finger. "To ask people with almost no money to pay for them?" she said. "The ones who need the gospel the most are often the ones who simply can't pay."

Another worker looked up from his desk. "I'll tell you a way that idea would save us money. We wouldn't have to spend time keeping accounts for the tax office!"

"See?" said Joy. "There we go. The gospel is free, and these records will be free too."

Joy had said it, so that's what happened.

What about when there wasn't enough money? What about when they had made the records and packed them, but they didn't have money to buy the postage to send them out?

They never asked anyone for money. So they started looking around to see how they could save a little here and a little there.

But the main thing they did was rejoice and pray. "Thank You, Lord, for all You've done. Thank You for all You're going to do! We look forward to seeing it!"

And they waited for the Lord to provide. And He always did.

After a year had gone by, the whole team gathered around the accounting books. "Look at this," said the accountant. He pointed to rows and columns of numbers. "Do you see this?"

Joy and the others looked.

"Gospel Recordings has finished the year without any debt at all!"

"That's how we always do it," Joy said. "If we don't have money, we don't buy anything. We always wait for the Lord to provide."

"But do you see why this is important?" asked the accountant.

They squeezed in to look closer.

"Gospel Recordings has produced almost twice as many records as before! Even with taking one day off a week for prayer!"

Joy clapped her hands. "That's the Lord!" she said. "I knew He could do it."

∂∽∂

Not long after, Joy and Ann made a four-thousand-mile trip to Alaska and recorded twenty-one more tribal languages. By 1949, when Gospel Recordings was ten years old, they had recorded over two hundred languages. Every one of them gave the amazing story of the gospel of Jesus Christ to someone who had never heard.

Chapter 8

To the Philippines!

"Well, it's farewell to the Hawaiian Islands," said Joy, leaning over the rail of the ship one fine day in 1949, waving good-bye to no one in particular. "And before long it will be hello to the Philippines. I can hardly wait!" She gazed out at the ocean in satisfaction. "It was wonderful, wasn't it, Ann? The Lord worked in everyone before we left home. Everybody made things right with everybody else and then the Lord gave blessings again." She sighed. "Oh, the Word of God is true, and how I wish everybody in the world knew it!"

"I do too," said Ann. She held the rail and turned to Joy. "Joy, I thought of something that I'm afraid you may not have thought of."

"What's that? We have everything. Our tickets, our passport, enough money, all the equipment for recording. . . ."

Ann hesitated. Then she blurted out, "I believe we forgot to write to anyone in the Philippines to ask for someone to meet us at the dock when we get there."

Joy gazed at her, open-mouthed. *How could they have forgotten such an important thing?*

"If there's no one there to meet us," Ann continued, "then we won't know where to go, and we can't speak the language—"

"And the government officials might take advantage of us. They might charge us even more than we have for all the equipment we're bringing into their country," Joy added. "But we will *not* worry! Ann, this is just GRP!"

"Yes, it definitely is that!" Ann replied. "Good Rejoicing Practice!"

"I don't know how we could have done such a thing as to forget," Joy continued, "but we will not worry about this. There's nothing we can do about it anyway. So it would do absolutely no good to worry, right? What am I saying? It never does any good to worry! We'll rejoice, right, Ann? Thank You, Lord! Thank You for GRP!"

"We'll rejoice," Ann agreed. "Maybe we didn't know what we were doing, but God always knows what He's doing. Thank You, Lord."

Through the rest of the voyage to the Philippines, Ann and Joy encouraged each other. If one of them began to worry or doubt, the other one would say, "We're trusting the Lord and rejoicing. We know He will carry us through. Thank You, Lord!"

Finally they saw the Philippine Islands loom on the horizon. The ship drew closer and closer. "You'll make a way for us, Lord," Joy murmured. "You make a pathway in the wilderness."

"We're on a mission for You, Lord. We're doing Your work," Ann prayed. "You will make the way clear."

The ship docked. Joy and Ann walked down the ramp to the dock. Then they saw an American man frantically waving his hat—at them.

Where had he come from?

"Miss Ridderhof? Miss Sherwood?" he said. "I'm Robert Bowman, at your service. I'll take care of all your baggage and take you back to the school where I work. You can stay there while you're in the Philippines."

Joy burst out laughing. "We knew the Lord would take care of us," she said, "but how did He send you?"

"Just this morning," Robert answered, "I received a letter from someone named Virginia Miller."

"Virginia!" Ann cried. "Virginia works with Gospel Recordings! She wrote to you?"

"Yes, she probably wrote it a couple of weeks ago. She explained the important work you'll be doing here and how you needed our help. So I just stopped everything I was doing and came straight out here to meet you."

"Isn't that just like the Lord," Ann murmured, shaking her head. "Taking care of us when we forget to take care of ourselves."

"And," added Joy, "giving us GRP."

❧❦

Ann and Joy spent hours in prayer together. They asked God where He wanted them to work first. There were hundreds of tribes in the Philippines, and so many missionaries asking for help! Finally they believed they knew the way God wanted them to go. Then the next thing to do was to ask Him for a car to take them there.

"You young men," Joy said to the students at the school where she and Ann were staying, "keep your eyes open for a car coming here for us. We've made our request for one."

The young men laughed. But a few days later, there was the car. A missionary told the students, "The Lord wants me to lend this car to Miss Ridderhof for her recording trip." And that was that.

With great thanksgiving, Joy and Ann loaded all their heavy recording equipment into the car.

They began to drive up the steep mountain trails to the villages.

Missionaries were glad to meet them. The tribal people were glad to see them. Everything was going very well.

Except one thing.

The recording equipment wouldn't work!

The huge machines with all their little parts—Joy and Ann couldn't get them working. They spent three weeks in the mountains of the Philippines. But they were able to make only one record.

The tiny voice of doubt began to whisper. *Why, Lord, why? We're here to do Your work!*

"Well, remember, this is GRP," Ann said. And together the two ladies rejoiced that God was over all.

"Ann, I remember a Bible story," said Joy. "Do you remember King Jehoshaphat? When he had to go out against the enemy, he sent singers ahead. They rejoiced that God was going before them to win the battle."

"I remember that," said Ann.

"This is a battle for us," said Joy. "A spiritual battle. We're going out against the powers of darkness. But there is much to gain. God won that battle for Jehoshaphat. And then the people took three days to bring in all the spoils of war!"

"There are a lot of tribes out there who need the gospel," Ann said.

"Yes," said Joy. "Those tribes are our spoils of war. We're fighting a battle. Prayer and rejoicing are our weapons. We can't forget that."

But they drove back down the mountain with only one recording, feeling discouraged.

The Bible school students looked over the recording equipment. "Never mind, we can fix this," they said. And they got it working perfectly.

Back up the mountain the women drove, praising and rejoicing. Within just a few days, they had the gospel story recorded in ten different languages.

అంటే

"So . . . we have to go to Mindoro next?" Joy and Ann looked at each other. The missionaries in the other three areas of the Philippines couldn't have them just yet.

Mindoro was an area with several tribal groups up in the hills. But there were no missionaries there. If they went to Mindoro, they would have to go without any American guides.

"Let's study the map," one of the men began. "That will give us some direction."

"I really can't study a map just yet," Joy answered. "There's no use in studying a map unless I know for sure what the Lord wants us to do. I have to pray. I need to just read my Bible and pray. I know you think I'm always hopping off like a jackrabbit for our next adventure. But right now I just need to seek the Lord."

Joy spent days reading her Bible and praying. "Is this what You want us to do, Lord? How will You lead us? What will we do? How will we manage all the heavy recording equipment on those mountain trails where we can't drive? You know it weighs a hundred and fifty pounds!"

As Joy read and prayed by the hour, she kept expecting the Lord to answer her. Then in Exodus 23:20 she read, "Behold, I send an angel before thee, to keep thee in the way, and to bring thee into the place which I have prepared."

"That's it!" she whispered. Then she called, "Ann! We have our answer! The Lord is going to send an angel before us!"

Chapter 9

God Makes a Way

The two women began gathering all the things they would need to go into the mountains, even though they didn't know anyone and couldn't speak the language.

But that recording equipment. Ugh. How in the world would they ever manage it on their own? It was huge and heavy and easily broken. They would have to carry it all themselves. And maybe someone would steal it. . . .

But then a package arrived.

"What is it?" Joy and Ann opened the package with wonder. It was sent by two men who had gone to work at the Gospel Recordings office back in California. They were wonderful men, brilliant men. They could fix anything. They could even invent things. . . .

Was this a new invention? A small metal box, about the size of a shoebox. Obviously some sort of equipment. Ann read the note that came with it. "We made this ourselves. We hope it will be useful."

It couldn't be. . . . It couldn't be. . . . Was it *recording equipment?* Was this small box going to replace the huge equipment that weighed a hundred and fifty pounds?

Joy and Ann followed the instructions and pressed the buttons. Ann spoke clearly into the machine. "Chief of Sky made all sky and earth and all people and all things in sky and earth."

She hit another button and heard her voice speaking it back to her.

"It works!" Joy cried. "It works perfectly! Maybe Al and Herman are some of the angels the Lord has sent!"

"They didn't come, though. This machine is what came. It's an angel machine!" Ann felt almost giddy with happiness. "Angel means *messenger*, right? This machine will carry the message. Look how easy it will be to carry!"

"Why, I can hold that under my arm!" Joy said. "It couldn't possibly be easier!"

That machine wasn't the only angel God sent. The Lord brought them to first one helper and then another. Finally they were led to a Christian family in Mindoro, Mr. and Mrs. Sulit and their many children. "How can we help you?" they asked.

Those were beautiful words to Joy. She explained about the work of Gospel Recordings. "We want to make a recording with the tribal people who live way up in those mountains."

Mr. Sulit shook his head. "I'm sorry, but we almost never see those tribal people. We don't see them even in the dry season. Now it's the rainy season. So we can be sure they won't come to the village."

"Oh, but we've asked God to send them," Joy said vigorously. "And we believe He will."

"We need to all keep our eyes open for them," Ann added.

All the children of the family ran to the windows of the little house and scanned the rainy horizon. After an hour, one of them cried, "There they are! There they are!"

Sure enough, two tribal boys had come down from the mountain to try to do some trading. One of them spoke a little of the main language of the Philippines.

Mr. Sulit invited the two teenage boys in for

food. And with that shoebox-size recording equipment, Ann began the recording process.

Joy spoke. Mr. Sulit spoke. Then one of the boys spoke.

"Chief of Sky sent message to all people of earth."

"This message came in bundle of leaves that Chief of Sky says."

"Bundle of leaves from Chief of Sky tell how all people are very bad."

The two boys seemed puzzled when they heard their own voices. But they stayed on and kept recording.

By the end of it, Joy had the whole gospel story finished. She was ready to make records to send to Mr. Sulit to use for the tribal people.

"God did this," she exclaimed triumphantly. "He sent angel guides and did it all."

ॐॐ

More time passed. Joy and Ann were with another missionary in another part of the Philippines.

The missionary, Mr. Spottswood pointed to a large map of the Philippines. "I flew over six thousand feet of mountains to get to that tribe of little people," he said. "They live way up there in the mountains. I want to start a medical mission up there with them. I would love to have some of your gospel recordings with me when I do."

"We absolutely have to get to them," Joy said with determination. "There has to be a way."

"That would be wonderful," Mrs. Spottswood said. "But there are no roads for cars, only foot paths. It takes five days of hiking uphill to get to them. I'm afraid it will be impossible."

"O Lord, make a way!" Joy and Ann prayed. "For Your glory! We praise You!"

One day when Ann was driving some Christian Filipino ladies around in the car, she suddenly asked, "Do any of the little people of the mountain tribes ever come here to town?"

"Oh yes," said one of the Filipino ladies. "They hike here to town about once a month."

Ann's heart began to sing.

"In fact," the lady continued, "some of them came just last Sunday, but of course they're gone now. They're very fearful. They come just to get what they need, and then they disappear."

Ann's heart began to sink.

But then one of the women told her to stop her car. She saw them talk to an old man with no teeth. Then the old man went someplace and brought back a young boy wearing only a cloth around his waist. She watched them all talk. Then she saw the boy nod his head vigorously. His squiggly brown hair flopped up and down.

"This old man can speak the tribal language," the Filipino lady told Ann. "This boy is from the mountain tribe. They both say they'll be glad to come back to the house with you. They can help you make a recording."

Before long they were back at the house.

"Joy!" Ann whispered. "We did it! We did it!"

"You did it?" Joy whispered back. "That's one of the little people? Really?"

"Yes! Can't you tell?"

"How did you get him?" asked Joy. "Who's the old man?"

"He's someone who knows the Filipino language *and* the tribal language!" Ann whispered triumphantly. "He's here to help!"

"Oh!" Joy breathed in wonder. "God has done something great here! Let's not waste a minute!"

Around the room in a circle they organized

themselves. Ann sat with the recording machine.

Then Joy spoke the words in English.

Then the Filipino lady translated the English words into the Filipino language.

Then the toothless old man translated the Filipino words into the tribal language.

Then the teenage boy spoke the words clearly in the tribal language into a microphone.

One sentence after another they spoke. Hour after hour.

The teenage boy spoke words that were new to him.

"Chief of Sky have great love for all people."

"Chief of Sky send His Son, His only one Son, to come to earth."

"He come to earth to receive punishment that should be ours."

The boy spoke each sentence into the microphone. Then Ann played it back to make sure it had been recorded well.

Every time—he heard a voice speaking his own language!

Every time—the voice spoke what he had just said!

Every time—he burst out laughing! He fell over backward in his wide-eyed amazement.

Every time—they had to help him get back up again and sit back down on his stool.

But bit by bit the whole story of the gospel was recorded.

"It's done! It's done! Praise God!" the ladies rejoiced together when the recording was finished.

"When Mr. Spottswood moves into the mountain tribes, he'll have his records in the tribal language!" Joy said. "God did it again!"

Chapter 10

Good Rejoicing Practice

"Well, it's the rainy season." Mr. Sosa. The Filipino pastor, looked out the window and shrugged.

Yes, it definitely was. In the Philippines there were only two seasons: dry and wet. Joy and Ann had done all the work they could in the Philippines during the dry time. And now, the rain beat down in torrents.

Mr. Sosa added, "If it weren't raining, I could take you over to that island. Someone there would speak the tribal language you want to record. But it's been raining for weeks."

Joy thought about George Mueller. He had once prayed for good weather in order to be able to go where he needed to go. He was right on the ship in a storm when he prayed it. Joy could do the same.

"Please find a boat for us, Mr. Sosa," she said. "God will make a way for us to get over there to the island."

Suddenly she realized that what she had said may have sounded foolish. "Let's pray right now, and ask Him to do it," she added. She closed her eyes and folded her hands. "O Lord, we know that You want that tribe to hear the gospel of Your Son Jesus in their very own language. You know that the only way for us to do it is to cross over to that island. You know that we can't do that until the rain stops. So we trust You to stop the rain. And we praise You. We praise Your

Name for what You're going to do! Thank You, Lord! We rejoice in You! Amen!"

Joy opened her eyes and looked around the room. Ann looked expectant. Mr. and Mrs. Sosa looked surprised. "Amen," Mr. Sosa said quietly.

The next morning Joy awoke early, remembering her prayer. "You are the one who works the miracles, Lord God," she prayed silently. "We praise You and rejoice in You!" She quietly crept from her bedroom to the window and peeked out.

The rain still fell steadily, the sky covered with dark clouds.

"Well then," she said. "This is simply GRP."

She returned to her bedroom and went down on her knees beside her bed for her Good Rejoicing Practice. "Lord!" she whispered. "I praise You for what You're going to do!"

Within a few hours, the sky was completely clear and the waters were calm. Joy and Ann rejoiced and prepared to leave for the island to make their next recording.

৵৶

"We're so glad to have you," Mr. Sutherland, the missionary, said. He spoke with enthusiasm in his Scottish accent, rubbing his hands together in satisfaction. "We've been praying about your coming for many months. We've been preparing for you. We dreamed of the day you would be here."

"Yes," added Mrs. Sutherland. "We haven't been here long, so we're still learning the tribal language, don't you know. But a young lady helped me translate some of our good hymns into the language. Some of the people are ready to sing them for you to record!" She laughed with delight.

"That's wonderful!" Joy beamed. "We've had some trouble with our recording equipment lately, but the Lord always gets it working somehow! It's all Good Rejoicing Practice."

"We call it GRP," Ann added, laughing.

Mr. and Mrs. Sutherland marveled at the small box that the ladies used in their recording. "All of it happens in something this small?"

"Yes, eventually," Joy answered. "Sometimes we have to slap it and knock it around and rejoice for quite a while first. But it always works sooner or later. The Lord has a job for us to do, and we need this little box in order to be able to do it."

"It's a marvel," said Mrs. Sutherland. "Just to think that with this small box you can make recordings that can help people listen to the gospel in their own language. Just think of it!"

"We've been thinking of it!" Joy laughed. "How many languages have we recorded in the Philippines so far, Ann?"

"I don't remember right now, but it must be dozens," Ann answered. "And we're not through. After we finish here, we still have more places to visit."

"You're doing the Lord's work for sure," said Mr. Sutherland, shaking his head. "There must be spiritual forces against you."

"Oh, yes, we've had our share," Joy answered. "But God is bigger. He always comes through."

The next morning Joy and Ann walked with Mr. Sutherland to the little chapel. The small building was crowded with people. They were all eager to see the American women who were going to record their voices. They were all excited to watch the recording process.

Joy stood with the Sutherlands as Ann began to set up the equipment. Then Ann's face suddenly frowned with concern. She turned the machine upside down and opened it. She took pieces out and put them back in.

"Is something wrong?" Mr. Sutherland whispered.

"Oh probably," Joy chuckled quietly. "We often have this kind of trouble at first. It's a test, I believe. But it will start working after a bit. It always does."

They waited and watched as Ann continued to study the machine and try different things.

"We've prayed for so many months . . ." Mr. Sutherland began.

"We'll just keep rejoicing for what the Lord is going to do!" Joy replied.

Ann worked on the machine for hours. The people in the chapel became restless and finally went home. Joy tried to help by continuing to rejoice. The Sutherlands tried to hide their disappointment and prayed.

But the machine was broken.

For two weeks Ann and Joy stayed in that part of the Philippines. Every day, praying and rejoicing, they tried the machine again. It never did start working.

The people had learned the songs. A man had prepared to speak the words of life into the microphone. But the machine never worked.

The last day they were there was a Sunday. Joy spoke to the people through a translator. "In the story of Lazarus," she said, "Mary was very sad because Lazarus had died. But Jesus said, 'I told you that if you would believe, you would see the glory of God.' The same is true for us. If we will believe, we will see the glory of God."

She looked out over the beach, to the ocean. They had come so far. They had tried so hard. The missionaries had prepared with so much prayer. Would they really have to leave with no recordings? How could it be?

But they would rejoice.

The next day the missionaries said goodbye with tears. Joy and Ann wanted to cry too.

But Joy was determined. As she sat on the ship going back up the coast, she wrote in her diary. "We're learning more about spiritual warfare. We still have many opportunities to rejoice."

On that very ship, Joy and Ann met a man who was able to help them find a teenage boy from that very same tribe in a school up the coast. There were also three girls from that same tribe in another school up the coast.

Joy and Ann arrived in a town where someone could fix their equipment. Then they found the teenage boy. He spoke the stories beautifully for the recording.

Then they found the girls. "Oh yes, we know those songs Mrs. Sutherland taught us!" they said. They sang the songs beautifully for the recording.

"We have them!" Joy wrote to the Sutherlands. "Recordings done! Records will be shipped to you soon! God has done His great work!"

❧

Joy and Ann stayed in the Philippines for a year. When they returned to Los Angeles in 1950, they had recorded the gospel in over ninety of the Philippines' tribal languages. Over half of these people groups had no Bible and had never before heard the gospel story.

Chapter 11

The Tribe No One Could Reach

Joy and her two friends, Ann and Sanna, sat in the jeep behind Mr. and Mrs. Ward, the missionaries. Also in the jeep were an African pastor, and three little men.

The three little men were each only about four feet tall. But they carried with them arrows and bows that were seven feet tall.

Across the wide open spaces of Africa the jeep bumped along, where there were no roads at all. Underneath their tires was not a long gray strip of highway. Instead, they bumped over small scrub bushes, dry sand, rocks, and cactus plants. Every once in a while the jeep hit a large rock that made them jolt around. But it kept going. And they kept going.

"Look! The zebra!" Joy pointed. The others watched as a whole herd of black and white striped beauties galloped across the savanna.

"Oh!" they all gasped together. Graceful impalas that had been grazing in front of them began to leap and bound into the distance. "So beautiful!"

"Look! A little dik-dik!" one of them called.

"They're as common as squirrels around here," said Joy, "but I just don't get tired of seeing them."

The jeep bounced along, mile after mile. Joy thought over the exciting events that had brought them to this place—with these three little men. One of them was even the chief of this mysterious little tribe.

৵৩

It was 1955. Joy, Ann, and Sanna had already been in East Africa for a year. They had recorded one tribal language after another. So many tribal people marveled to hear the news of salvation in their own language coming out of a box! So many missionaries expressed their great gratitude! Day after day was filled with rejoicing.

But then they had found out about the little Kindiga people. Very short people, and a very small and secret tribe.

"No missionary has been able to reach them yet," someone said.

"But elephant hunters love to hire them if they can," the missionary had explained back in the mission house. "They can hold a bow that's seven feet tall. When they fire that arrow, they never miss!"

This tribe was a very small group of people,

103

and hard to get to. The ladies determined that they simply had to make a recording for them. So they began to pray that God would bring them the people to record.

And He had.

Mr. Ward had been able to find these same three little men, with their seven-foot high bows. They had come to the mission house and worked for days to make recordings for their people. The ladies had organized themselves for recording as they'd done many times before.

Mrs. Ward had translated from English to Swahili. The African pastor translated from Swahili to the other African language. The Kindiga chief and the other two men had listened to the words in a language they understood. Then they spoke it into the box in their own language. The old chief had "taught" the box, shaking his finger at it.

And now they had a stack of eight precious records ready to play on the mysterious box for the Kindiga tribe. Stories of the love of God for all men and women and children. Stories that tell that everyone from all over the world needs Jesus Christ for salvation.

❦

"Looks like this is as far as we can go," Mr. Ward said. The jeep pulled up to the edge of a steep river bank.

The little men pointed into the distance, to a hill two miles away.

"That's where their tribe is," the African pastor explained.

All nine people climbed out of the jeep and began to carefully work their way down the river bank and across the almost-dry riverbed. "Look out for rhinos here," the African pastor said. "Elephants too. They can show up any time."

"Look!" Joy called. "There they go!" She pointed to the three little men. They scrambled up the far side of the river bed and bounded off over the land on the other side. They ran at top speed back to their homes, far from strange houses with strange black boxes.

"Can we find the way without them?" Ann asked.

"Yes," said the African pastor. "It's at the top of that hill where they pointed. If we hurry, we can get there before dark."

They moved as quickly as they could through the undergrowth. But still, it was dark when they arrived at the little village.

Some of the people knew a few words of Swahili.

"Jambo, Mama!" one called shyly.

"Jambo, Bwana!" said another carefully.

By the light of the torches the missionaries entered the dark little village. There they saw the men, many children, and women with babies slung over their backs. They saw young people with headbands of woven grass.

As they climbed the hill to the village, the missionaries heard the little old chief talking to the people.

"Their language is such a fascinating mystery," Joy whispered to Ann. "Clicks and pops and trills, like forest creatures."

A hyena wailed somewhere far away. Joy felt a shiver go up her spine. What a strange world this was!

A few little fires glowed in the middle of the cluster of huts. The flames cast a strange red glow on the black faces. Before long all the missionaries were seated on flat rocks under a giant baobab tree, the center of the entire village.

107

One of the ladies held a flashlight. Mr. Ward gently set the record player on a low stone. He pulled out the eight precious records they had made with the chief.

It was time. Time in this little village far from all civilization to play the true story that never grows old. It was the story of the great God and His Son, the Savior Jesus Christ, a story these tribal people had never heard.

The little people sat in complete silence. They watched as the missionary carefully took the player arm of the record player and put it on the record.

They listened. They gasped. It was the chief's voice! The chief was talking to them in their own language from that black box!

"My Kindiga people, for many years our fathers have not known the true God. They worshiped false gods and evil spirits. No one told them the truth about these things. But now we have the light. Listen to the Good News of the true God who loves us!"

Joy, Ann, and Sanna couldn't see the faces of the little people in the dark. But they could hear the clicks and pops of this mysterious language as the little people quietly expressed their astonishment.

"Hear these words about God's Son, Jesus Christ," said the voice from the record in the tribal language. "He lived on this earth as a Man. He died to pay for our sins. But He arose again from the dead and is living now in Heaven. He will forgive the sins of all who believe in Him."

The strange voice continued out of the little box. All eyes were fixed on it. Even the old chief watched it. He was the one who had spoken those words into the microphone only a few hours before. That was very far away from these stones in a dark village under a baobab tree.

"My people, will you also follow the light? Do you want eternal life from God? Put your trust in Jesus Christ. Ask Him to forgive your sins. Obey His words. When this life is over, it is Jesus who will take you to Heaven."

Ann carefully took out her camera and snapped a photograph of the people in the dark. When her camera flashed, all the missionaries could see the deep concentration on the faces of the people. They sat still, in wonder.

"There is only one true God. It is He who created us. He loves us. He gave us salvation through His Son. He wants us to follow Him and worship Him only. He gives forgiveness and peace to those who believe in Jesus. He will fill our hearts with joy. He will care for us as a Father cares for His children."

One record after another. Each time the people asked for more.

"Jesus Christ," the voice on the last record said over and over. That was the name of the Savior. "Jesus Christ." They worked hard to get their tongues around the strange sounds.

"God is calling everyone. He calls fathers and mothers. He calls children and elders. He calls rich and poor. Let us all give Him our hearts. Let us serve Him. Let us praise Him for Jesus Christ and His many gifts to us!"

The people sat in silence for a few moments, thinking.

"Sawa, sawa," said the old chief. The women bowed their heads. They knew he was saying, "It is right, it is right."

"Sawa, sawa," repeated the little people.

Joy looked around in the darkness, at the dim firelight, the dim outline of the record player. She listened to the strange sounds of the African jungle.

It was a different world. But the truth was the same.

"Sawa, sawa," she echoed back. "It is right."

Chapter 12

Follow the Jericho Pattern

In 1963, Joy Ridderhof turned sixty years old. Gospel Recordings was known all over the world. They had offices in Canada, England, Australia, Africa, and India. Several young adults were now traveling the world to record languages as Joy and Ann had once done. "Remember," Joy told them, "the missionaries who live in the countries learn the main languages. Our job is to catch the languages of the little tribes, the ones where no one has gone yet. That's where God has called us."

Now Joy was invited to speak in churches and conferences all over the country, and in other countries too. How was God answering prayer in Gospel Recordings? How has He called us to rejoice in trial? People loved listening to Joy speak.

One day when she was traveling and speaking, the staff at Gospel Recordings sent her a message: They were going to buy some property to build their new office—the old office was so full and crowded!—but now the deadline was near and they didn't have enough money. They still needed over thirty thousand dollars. And the deadline was only a week away.

What a lot of money! What a short time!

"Follow the Jericho pattern," Joy said into the telephone. "Tell everyone who works with Gospel Recordings to follow the Jericho pattern. Don't tell anyone else about our need."

The staff had been working with Joy long enough to know what she meant. For two hours every afternoon, all the people who worked at Gospel Recordings in seven countries met for prayer. They had seven days to pray for God to bring down this wall that kept them from getting the property they needed.

Joy was traveling and speaking. But she stopped for prayer for two hours every afternoon as well.

They prayed, and they rejoiced. They trusted God to provide.

But it certainly was a lot of money!

The first, second, and third days went by. No money came in.

On the fourth day, Joy read the story of Jericho in the book of Joshua. She saw the verse that said, "In three days you will pass over this river and go in and possess the land."

Back in Los Angeles, the staff read the same verse. They felt sure too.

There was no money. But God would provide.

The next day, the fifth day, a call came from the office in England. "A Christian lady here has died. She left a large inheritance to Gospel Recordings. We're sending it all to the office in California!" It was even more than the thirty thousand dollars they needed.

The staff praised God and bought the property. Joy went on to speak in church after church. She told them how their very own walls of Jericho had fallen.

க்ஷ்

In 1964, Gospel Recordings celebrated its twenty-fifth anniversary. By that time, the missionaries had recorded the story of the true

God and His Son Jesus Christ in *over three thousand languages.*

In 1965, when Joy was 62 years old, she made another trip through Central America. This time a young man went as her companion.

"Oh, Jim," she said, beaming, "I can hardly wait to get down to Honduras! I haven't seen my friends there for twenty-five years—think of it! Why, I wasn't much older than you when I first went down there!"

The young missionary smiled at the older lady's enthusiasm.

"But mainly," she continued, "we'll chase down as many hidden tribes as we can, you know. We have these hand-crank record players now! We can just leave them there for them to play the records over and over. God is doing so much!"

They did succeed in giving the gospel to people who had never heard it in their own language, sometimes in very dangerous territory.

On this trip they were able to go to the little village of Marcala in Honduras.

"I have lots of friends here," Joy explained to Jim. "We've been writing letters back and forth for all these years. Oh! I can't wait to see Don Pedro!" She clapped her hands in excitement.

As they arrived, Joy gasped and pointed. "Look! They're having a meeting in the chapel!" At every window they saw colorful scarves and hats. All the Christians were gathered together!

After the meeting they gathered around her. "Miss Joy! Miss Joy!" some said, just like the old days. These were her spiritual children. Now her spiritual children had spiritual children of their own. Joy was a spiritual grandmother!

"Come speak! Come speak!" they called.

Joy stood up in front of the little chapel to speak of the goodness of God and the love and joy of Jesus. Tears ran down her cheeks.

Some people in the little chapel didn't know who she was. But when others whispered the story—"she brought the good news to us!"—they beamed with smiles too. It was a great time to rejoice over what God had done.

"But where is Don Pedro?" Joy asked, anxious.

"He'll be back tomorrow night," they promised.

The next morning would be Sunday. "Jim," Joy said hesitantly, "the Lord is telling me that I need to go to a little village farther up the mountain."

"I'm here to drive you wherever you need to go," Jim answered.

They left at 7:00 in the morning. Jim drove the car as far as he could. Finally, though, the road became too narrow, so they had to get out and walk. "Are you sure you want to do this?" Jim asked, concerned for the older lady.

"Yes," Joy answered with determination. "The Lord is telling me He wants me to visit this village."

Hours later, they finally arrived. Here they met a few Christians who had been meeting together to worship. Joy introduced herself and explained who she was.

"Do you remember me?" asked one man.

Joy looked at him. "Uh . . ."

He continued. "When you were just a young woman, you went to visit prisoners in the jail in the capital city. It was Christmas, and you brought gifts. I was in that jail, and I listened to you giving the Good News. It was the first time I had ever heard it. I had heard of Jesus, of course. But I didn't know about His Good News of free salvation till then. I trusted in Jesus that day."

Someone else added, "He came back here to his home from the jail, and he was a different person! He just talked about Jesus. Many of us have believed in Christ because of him."

That afternoon Joy and Jim traveled back down the mountain. As they walked, they rejoiced together.

They arrived in Marcala in time for the evening meeting. There was Don Pedro! Joy and Don Pedro embraced each other with tears. Then they prayed together.

Don Pedro said, "We have some good preachers in our country today. Some of the main ones were trained in your Bible school here in Marcala thirty years ago. God has given great fruit from your ministry here."

Finally the two missionaries drove away. Joy felt as if her heart would burst with happiness. "Well, Jim," she finally said, "I think that even news about our gospel recordings couldn't make me any more full of joy than I am right now. It seems like almost too much joy! Marcala, a Christian village! My six years there weren't wasted, no, not at all. God was at work. He made the little seeds that were planted bear much fruit."

Epilogue

By the 1960s, Gospel Recordings centers had been set up in many different countries around the world.

Many other people came to join the work. Many helped to make recordings in other countries. But Joy still traveled all over and spoke in churches and Bible schools and conferences. She wanted all people to know the great things God was doing through the little black records and the little cassette tapes that the people of Gospel Recordings were giving away for free.

Explorers and missionaries explored the jungles and mountains of the world. They found more and more small tribes. This meant there were more languages than they thought. Some people guessed that there were over nine thousand languages and dialects in the world.

Joy died in 1984 when she was 81 years old. But the mission of Gospel Recordings lives on. Now its name has been changed to Global Recordings. Workers continue to record stories of the gospel of Jesus Christ in all the languages of the world. So far, they have recorded over six thousand of them.

Now they use DVDs and MP3 players. But the work is the same. People all over the world are hearing the gospel for the first time. They can rejoice with Joy Ridderhof in the great things God has done. In all different languages, they praise the Name of the One who gave us His Son, Jesus Christ.

About the Author

Rebecca Davis lives in Greenville, South Carolina, where her home hosts many guests for quiet cups of coffee or big jolly parties. She and her husband, Tim, have finished 25 years of homeschooling and are now watching their four grown children forge their own paths in following Jesus Christ.

Researching, writing, and speaking fill more of her time as Rebecca develops the Potter's Wheel series of Christian biographies for children and the Hidden Heroes series of true missionary stories for children and families. At her website, *www.hiddenheroesmissionarystories.com*, you can see her books, storytelling presentations, and other information.

*Learn More about the Hidden Heroes series
of True Missionary Stories
published by Christian Focus Publications*

෨ᅠᅠᅠ෨

Hidden Heroes Missionary Stories
true stories of God at work around the world

by Rebecca Davis

The wind of the Spirit of God has been blowing around the world to draw people to Himself . . . through Africa . . . Asia . . . South America . . . island nations . . . the Middle East . . . the Far East . . . and on and on around the world.

The Hidden Heroes series of true missionary stories tells these true stories of the work of God through little-known Western missionaries and through the national Christians of the lands . . . over the last two hundred years, and up to the present day.

Written on the upper-elementary level, but with adults in mind too, the Hidden Heroes series is designed for family read-alouds and classroom discussions.

See *www.hiddenheroesmissionarystories.com* for Educator Resources for each book, including coloring pages, handwriting pages, activity pages, background information, and links to photos and videos.

Hidden Heroes #1

With Two Hands
Stories of God at Work in Ethiopia

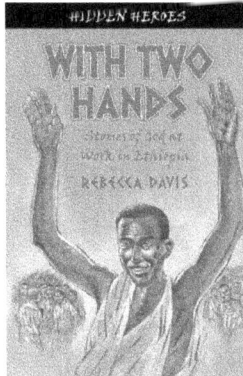

Why would a slave and a witch doctor walk for three days to find the white man called Jesus? Why would a crippled old man wait by the side of the road every day for twenty years? Why would a lame man purposely walk to a tribe where he knew he could be killed?

Written on the upper-elementary level, sixteen true missionary stories taken from the ministry of one missionary show the power of God in the midst of darkness, among people of Ethiopia who saw the great light of the gospel. Published 2010 by Christian Focus Publications. For more information, see the website *www.hiddenheroesmissionarystories.com*.

Hidden Heroes #2

The Good News Must Go Out
Stories of God at Work
in the Central African Republic

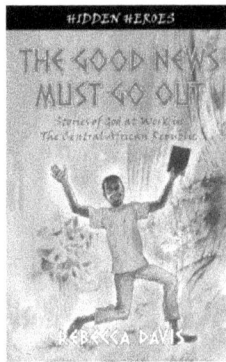

A sultan whose 300 wives were buried alive . . . cannibals who believed there was no such thing as a white woman . . . an elegant French lady who watched in horror as the missionary performed surgery on her kitchen table.

These are just a few of the real people encountered in these true missionary stories of Margaret Nicholl Laird in her ministry in the Central African Republic, as she and many others gave their lives in service of the King of Glory, whose Good News could not be stopped. Published 2011 by Christian Focus Publications.

Hidden Heroes #3

Witness Men: True Stories of God at Work in Papua, Indonesia

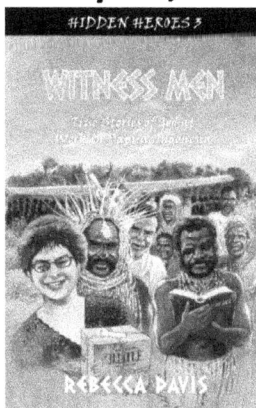

In 1938, in the remote highlands of a mountainous island, explorers discovered thousands upon thousands of tribal people. Missionaries began to come, to bring the Good News of the Gospel, to tell them about Jesus. Little did they know that many of the people of the tribes had been waiting . . . waiting . . . for someone to come and help them out of the darkness of their old way of life.

Fifteen chapters on the upper-elementary level tell the true missionary stories of the gospel spreading throughout the highlands of Papua, Indonesia, from 1955 to 2010, when one of the tribes received their first New Testaments. Published 2013 by Christian Focus Publications..

Hidden Heroes #4

Return of the White Book: True Stories of God at Work in Southeast Asia

When Adoniram Judson took the Gospel, the good news about the Lord Jesus, to the people of Burma in 1813, he didn't know that high up in the hills lived a tribe of people whose ancient stories and songs served as continual reminders that one day the White Book that their ancestors had lost would be brought back to them.

Sixteen chapters on the upper-elementary level tell stories of the transformation that the Word of God brought to the Hill Tribes of Southeast Asia. Published 2014 by Christian Focus Publications. For more information, see the website *www.hiddenheroesmissionarystories.com.*

Hidden Heroes #5

Lights in a Dark Place
True Stories of God at Work in Colombia

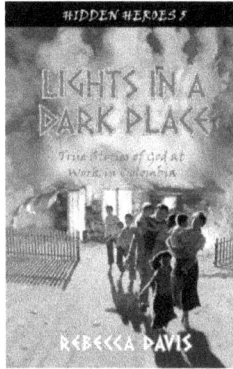

Colombia has been known as a land of violence, but God is at work! Even though the Colombian people have reacted with violence to the Gospel of Jesus Christ, God has delivered people from burning houses . . . God has healed ones who cursed . . . God has given people dreams and visions . . . God has rescued kidnapers . . . God has conquered demons of darkness. Read fourteen true stories of the Light of the World shining in the land of Colombia, South America. Published 2014 by Christian Focus Publications.

Hidden Heroes #6

Living Water in the Desert
True Stories of God at Work in Iran

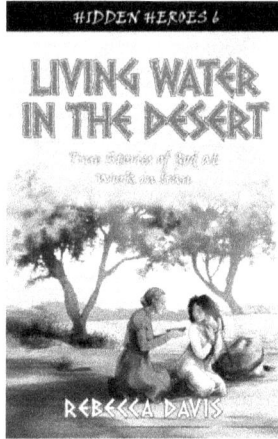

One man was overcome by the missionary's kindness. Another was stopped by a vision of men in blue. One became sick and tired of his own religion. Another saw a man named Jesus in a dream, coming to him on a donkey. A girl found a strange book on the floor of the library and visited a secret prayer meeting. Seventeen chapters tell true stories of the Living Water pouring out on the country of Iran. And it's still happening! The most recent story in this book is from 2013.

Read fourteen true stories of the Living Water pouring out on the land of Iran. Christian Focus Publications 2015.

Potter's Wheel #1

Fanny Crosby
Queen of Gospel Songs

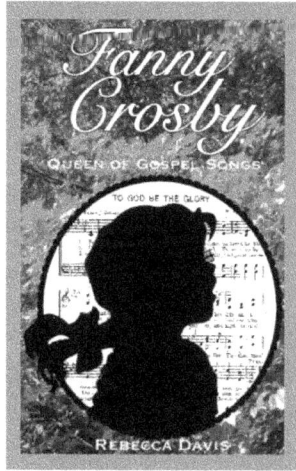

The man said he was a doctor . . . but he did something to little baby Fanny's eyes that made her blind for the rest of her life. How could she find out about the world around her? How could she be happy? How could she learn? How could she love God? How could she forgive?

Fanny Crosby was blind for more than ninety years . . . and she wrote over 8,000 hymns and gospel songs about her Savior.

Potter's Wheel Books are designed to show children the Master Potter at work through Christian biography for children ages 7-10.